ADVENTURES IN THE LOST INTERIORS OF AMERICA

CLEVELAND STATE UNIVERSITY POETRY CENTER
NEW POETRY

Michael Dumanis, Series Editor

Samuel Amadon, *The Hartford Book*
John Bradley, *You Don't Know What You Don't Know*
Lily Brown, *Rust or Go Missing*
Elyse Fenton, *Clamor*
Rebecca Hazelton, *Vow*
Rebecca Gayle Howell, *Render / An Apocalypse*
Emily Kendal Frey, *The Grief Performance*
Dora Malech, *Say So*
Shane McCrae, *Mule*
Helena Mesa, *Horse Dance Underwater*
Philip Metres, *To See the Earth*
Zach Savich, *The Firestorm*
Sandra Simonds, *Mother Was a Tragic Girl*
S. E. Smith, *I Live in a Hut*
Mathias Svalina, *Destruction Myth*
Allison Titus, *Sum of Every Lost Ship*
Liz Waldner, *Trust*
William D. Waltz, *Adventures in the Lost Interiors of America*
Allison Benis White, *Self-Portrait with Crayon*
Jon Woodward, *Uncanny Valley*
Wendy Xu, *You Are Not Dead*

For a complete listing of titles please visit
www.csuohio.edu/poetrycenter

ADVENTURES IN THE LOST INTERIORS OF AMERICA

POEMS BY
WILLIAM D. WALTZ

Cleveland State University Poetry Center
Cleveland, Ohio

First edition
5 4 3 2 1

This book is published by the
Cleveland State University Poetry Center,
2121 Euclid Avenue, Cleveland, Ohio 44115-2214
www.csuohio.edu/poetrycenter and is distributed by
SPD / Small Press Distribution, Inc. www.spdbooks.org.

Adventures in the Lost Interiors of America was
designed and typeset by Randall Heath in Cheltenham.

   Library of Congress Cataloging-in-Publication Data
Waltz, William D., 1960-
   [Poems. Selections]
   Adventures in the lost interiors of America :
   poems / by William D. Waltz. -- First edition.
      pages cm
   Includes bibliographical references and index.
   "Distributed by SPD / Small Press Distribution, Inc."--T.p. verso.
   ISBN 978-0-9860257-1-6 (paperback : acid-free paper)
      I. Title.
PS3623.A367A65 2013
811'.6--dc23   2013000068

ACKNOWLEDGMENTS

Sincere and grateful acknowledgment is made to the editors of the following publications in which these poems first appeared, sometimes with different titles or in slightly different forms:

Black Warrior Review: "Saint Anthony Falls," "Human Snack," and "Enough Light"

Court Green: "Waiting Room"

Denver Quarterly: "Future Structures"

Forklift, Ohio: "We Pilgrims Piggybacked the River, Instinct Puffy in Our Eyes," "Morning Ornithology," and "Collective Hum"

Glitterpony: "Calculus Accumulates Upon the Mighty Cuspids," "United Microclimates," "The Other Side," and "Prevailing Westerly"

H_NGM_N: "*Please*, She Said" and "What It Is That Abandons You"

jubilat: "I'll Be the One Wearing Tiny White Boots" and "Brian's Brain"

MiPoesias: "And Everything Else," "On the Warp Path," "A Part of It," "Birds, Still," and "Before We Begin"

National Poetry Review: "*Island in Dispute Disappears into the Sea*" and "Catch & Release"

POOL: "Falling Back into the Sky"

Rain Taxi: "A Continuing Education"

Washington Square: "A Little Stick" and "Letter to an Incomplete Stranger"

"Future Structures" was featured on *Poetry Daily*.

"Saint Anthony Falls," "Brian's Brain," and "*Island in Dispute Disappears into the Sea*" were featured on *Verse Daily*.

Under a different title, "Catch & Release" can be found in the anthology *Poetry City, USA, Vol. 2* (Lowbrow Press, 2012).

"We Pilgrims Piggybacked the River, Instinct Puffy in Our Eyes" appears in the anthology *Stories For Shorty: A Collection of Recollections from the Jockey Club 1982-1988* (Aurore Press, 2008). Thank you, Jockey Club, for bringing Dead Kennedys to the banks of the Ohio River when we needed them most.

Thanks are due Álvar Núñez Cabeza de Vaca whose life I admire and whose title I've abused.

Great full moon thanks go to Dara Wier and Factory Hollow Press for publishing *Confluence of Mysterious Origins*, a chapbook containing some of these poems.

I'd also like to thank Dobby Gibson, James Haug, Steve Healey, and Bob Hicok for their friendship and for bravely reading and commenting on this manuscript.

Thanks to Becca Barniskis, Kath Jesme, and Amy McNamara for exploring the renshi with me and for inspiring the poems I discovered along the way.

Much gratitude is due Randall Heath, a trailblazing book designer and a dear friend.

Thanks to Frank Giampietro for his close reading and true compass.

Thank you, Hart, for joining our adventure.

Thank you, Brett, for everything.

Lastly, humble thanks are due Cape Cod, Resurrection Bay, Pike Island, Lake Superior, Medicine Rock, Serpent Mound, Big Sur, Kilauea, the Everglades, the Mississippi River, Oregon, Idaho, Montana, and Ohio for giving my imagination direction.

FOR CLARK

CONTENTS

3

4

5

I shall collect plants and fossils and make astronomic observations. But that's not the main purpose of my expedition—I shall try to find out how the forces of nature interact upon one another. . . . In other words, I must find out about the unity of nature.

—Alexander von Humboldt, letter to a friend , 1799

I looked up and saw Japhy running down the mountain in huge twenty-foot leaps, running, leaping, landing . . . then taking another long crazy yelling yodelaying sail down the sides of the world and in that flash I realized it's impossible to fall off mountains.

—Jack Kerouac, *The Dharma Bums*

ADVENTURES IN THE LOST INTERIORS OF AMERICA

Before We Begin

Let's pause
on the pond's edge,
cattails rustling,
one against another,
like a field of crickets,
one seamless song.
Then a puny bubble
rushing to the surface
disturbs a sleeping water bug.
Let us praise the unknown
source lurking below, let's
appreciate how little we know,
how little what we know
matters—what bug?
Predacious diving beetle,
ubiquitous whirligig dead
still surfing a lazy Doppler?
Let's not sidetrack
to side effects of breathing
because there's another
bubble—something moved.
Snapper mouth agape?
Catfish garbling the blues?
I'm almost certain
we're not alone
when we pray
for something terrible
not to happen.
Could be methane,
percolating muck, plant
matter gone punk.
Creature from the Black

Lagoon, could be.
He rose from primordial
ooze like life itself,
like Martin Sheen
in the scene he unmerges
from the Mekong.
If we keep coming back
to death, like our walks
return us to the lake,
it's because death is nothing
without us. Rising up
through the dark broken water,
weed and water lily parting,
we begin, a gamble
with a face. Then
we move on.

Brian's Brain

The alien topographies
the brain displays
resemble stems of Caribbean coral
or the pockmarked surface of the moon,
which in turn resembles
Craters of the Moon
National Park—but that's comparing
two halves of one brain.
It can be flat in Idaho,
and where it is is sometimes stacked
with volcanic rock, piles of black books
forgotten among the library of trees.
Studies show the wind alone
courses the gorges and scours
the gulches of the Western desert,
our desiccated inland sea,
home to Atomic City,
poor Shoshone.
There is raven and crow,
eagle and sparrow,
and like pharaoh the radiant
vulture reigns over the earth
and its vast crevasses,
the furrowed flesh of gray matter.
If there is salt in our blood,
it's a vestige of the sea. If
there's mud in our marrow,
it's magma's memento. If
pottery chips and coral bits
litter the desert floor, then
there are more mirages than oases.
A vulture rides the thermals. Up
ahead, the sun.

Natural Science

Fish can drown,
fish can fly, even
though I haven't seen it.
Lucky birds swim.
Some call them ducks.
I watched a loon dive
down at dawn
on Independence Day
while the cabin dreamed.
Mammals can swim, too,
save gorillas,
giraffes, armadillos,
and the hippo
who walks underwater
like some kind of feral
Jesus. Imagine
a snorkeling elephant
delivers good news
just above the surface.
We can fly,
we flew to the moon
and planted the Stars
and Stripes. We haven't
returned and that's like
giving up on peaches
or friendship.
As a child I loved
Wild Kingdom and
the *Wonderful World*,
especially those episodes
where dogs and cats trekked
across exurbia to reunite

with human families.
I've always half-expected
incredible journeys,
since I learned to swim
in Resurrection Bay
and to love
swimming in a pool
that cradled me,
like a shy newt
in a great blue hand,
while I listened
to the water open
its secret heart,
which is what the loon
did at Green Lake
when the furtive bird
sent a pulse of ripples
across the water,
circles on a sonar screen,
that traveled up the dock,
up the fern path,
to the cabin, packed tight
with fog, and poured me out,
onto shore,
a pill of a man,
my feet soft
on the sandy bottom,
the gentle attention
of minnows, and then
the loon broke through
with its longing song
and unlocked the lake

and something in me
with its mystery note.
Although I couldn't see
beyond the dark spot bobbing
in the morning mist,
I knew the sun shone somewhere
and the far shore brandished
a stand of shining white birch.
There was nothing left
to do but dive in
before the smell of black
coffee and blueberry pie
reminded me how beautiful
and incomplete
my communion was
and would be until
it was no longer.

Waiting Room

We tried to be not disappointed.
We did.
We did the things
the oracle suggested
and then some. Then someone
suggested emptying our pockets
which was a non sequitur.
A non sequitur is an unexpected erection.
A sneeze is an exclamation point,
exclamation without feeling,
which is like a clock
without time.

Out of time we waited a little longer.
The walls were busy, very busy
with the business of man
which can be dirty business.
I tried calling the oracle.
The oracle wasn't answering
and may have jumped bail.
We weren't sure. We weren't sure
what would happen next,
but we promised not to be disappointed.
To be disappointed looks like a cormorant
when you expect a manatee.

Manatees have been mistaken
for mermaids by sailors.
Another name for manatee is sea cow.
Sea cows are fetching creatures
but I find it hard to be aroused.
I'm old-fashioned that way.

The way we plunged
our hands into our pockets
suggested plumbing and water
and water rising.
Hope and fear are like
flotsam, soft and ripe.
Accept what the flood rejects.
Reject the architecture surrounding
your wild beating heart. We changed.

We changed from well inside the outside.
We emptied our pockets and our purses.
Emptying our purses is another way of saying
the gibbous moon is time without a clock
and portends a joyous swelling.
The clock achieved convexity
while we waited. The nurse spoke,
her diphthongs deployed deliberately,
her stockings whispered.
We tried to be not what we weren't.
We tried to be not excited.
We listened and the words came.

The Other Side

Dear Earthling, a thin membrane
separates this world from its watery preface.
Did you hear me? I moved my lips
and said we share something with the fishes,
but that's no secret to astronauts like us.
Everything you've heard is true
regarding spring and the moon.
All else is subject to interpretation.
Hurry up might mean *I look forward
to the day we meet* to an expectant father
and *Watch out for the bright
lights of joy* to an aboriginal son.
I carried joy home once
and the crowd cheered.
Words divide us into tribes.
Some believe tribes
divide us into words.
I believe division has been perjured
by good intentions. After all,
life began when two cells fused
and then divided and divided
and divided.

Letter to an Incomplete Stranger

In the courtyard of the art institute you will find a small stand of birch trees and a dark, shining wave of periwinkle crashing against their majestic, frail white trunks. I'm sorry if the word periwinkle makes you uncomfortable. It's only a word and we mustn't be afraid of what we know. Between the surging groundcover and the brick façade separating present conditions from examples of Ife civilization, notice a squat, stone bench in the shade. One day one of us will read a famous Russian novel there. I wonder what Tolstoy would do. I'd like to imagine he'd write a better chapter to our end. I have explored your museum's mammoth collection, but if not for the docent I never would've discovered the piece that arouses me most, a small female figurine, found in France, carved from sandstone. A rough-hewn Venus dating back 22,000 years to the venue of Neanderthal's last stand in the wilderness we call the here and now. I'm amazed we ever lived with other *people*, neighbors with bigger brains, strangers missing fossil records. I feel certain we can again, coexist, I mean. You may not remember, but our eyes met once in a cool, wide pool of plate glass. I knew then I would never understand you completely, nor would I betray you by thinking I did.

The Eye in Sidewalk

Smoldering under the sick
gray snow of last month,
a billion tiny eruptions.
This is the street
that calls us home.

*

Take these poor potholes
as evidence of spring, and if
the red oaks refuse to drop
their royal robes before
the return of the grackles,
it's proof the sting of fall lasts
long after the first frost fades.

*

One Sunday
the tulips by the window
wore snow like bonnets
floating above the meadow.
We've all wandered through
the tall grass and found
a foot path leading
to some other other.

*

This street has many secrets
and I believe you're one.
For when the crickets confess

their loneliness to the twilight
blooming in your wake,
the trees nestle their limbs and
the sparrow whispers to the bee
before lining her nest
with the soft tufts of gossip.

Human Snack

There are days when it's gray

and the cold is a giant sock

that can't be escaped or even lost,

and brittle phalanges ache like icicles

shattering on the mall concourse.

There are also bad days,

days that just say no

when you wished they'd say of course

or excellent and absolutely.

Still the voluntary sparrows

call down from their perches

in the pet food store.

Not all animals lack

the capacity to appreciate

the absence of freedom.

Some spin their exercise wheels

between nibbles and naps in cotton

fluff—and that's enough.

The uninvited ornithology

defies the obvious

ideas of beauty and profit.

Their chatter suggests

our purchases patronize

a strange and soulless creature

gorging at the nexus of wonder

and loneliness. Like sparrows

we may exit whenever

the automatic doors swing

open. Till then we wander

the odd and even rows.

We pop the top off

the snake cage,

serenade the love birds,

and wish the spayed

and neutered set well.

The volunteers proclaim

we are part of a union,

a sacred union. We all join

together. We're customers,

just not good ones.

When we tap the glass,

an orange storm,

the comet school scatters.

Here Come the Segues

Somebody invented a people
mover and called it a segue.
A candle in a cave,
history is illuminating
and entertaining
on a people mover.
The queues at the mill
ruins teach us that.
I don't like to wait
for history or for dumplings
on a paper plate. There are
7,000,000,000 like me,
one in five is Chinese.
The tour begins at the falls
where hansom cabs wait,
in the shade of wild trees,
where the river says *flow*,
where the limestone bluffs
buffer light in yellow bowls.
The tour begins at the arches.
The arches with limestone
and men, men with dreams,
dreams of walking on water.
"The first bridge is a breakthrough,
the second, a conveyance" is
an old saying I made up today.
Khrushchev and Brezhnev
helped Mao bridge the Yangtze,
which is our Mississippi,
which is India's Ganges,
which is Russia's Neva.
The river moans like one rock crushing

another, while the city says *millstone*
and *sluice* and the people say *pumpernickel.*
The Saint of Lost Things
gave his name to the falls
and the falls gave a great spirit
a way to say goodbye.
The river begins north
of the need for a bridge.
The guide points to the cataracts
and says *catacombs* when a dead tree
floats by. Everyone looks
to see the edge.
Some rivers are mythological,
others, obstacles.
The guide assures the tourists
the empty space downstream
is the lost bridge of the North Star,
a bridge on its knees.
Even great rivers have modest beginnings
and may flow in any direction,
yet all follow a path of least resistance.
Lewis and Clark slogged 4,000 miles
upstream, looking for passage,
which proves people aren't rivers.
From Cape Disappointment, one sees
China, if one imagines it.
The people movers depart
down the Stone Arch Bridge,
like wild horses wandering off,
to witness the hiss of mill ruins
smoldering on the far bank.

Saint Anthony Falls

A language of snapping
twigs and smoke drifts
overhead, between the lindens
and the stupid streetlights.
The crows descend.
They drape the neighborhood
in a black net. They are a system.
Each bird a node, a hard knot
that dissolves at dusk.
An electric eye can be fooled
to believe day is night
by an outstretched wing.
On brittle winter afternoons
crows can be found
warming themselves like this,
silhouettes in prayer,
still as the snow that creaks
below. Their minds,
virgin forests of new ice.
It is evening. A murder has gathered.
The crows are about to change
everything.

Birds, Still

The woods walked through us and left a trail. We followed, down a street, over a hill, across a stream and a field, and then through a wood where we came upon a thicket rich with cricketsong and morning thorn. We peeled back the pricks and moved like herons through the reeds until an opening and then the prairie and across we saw a flock of silhouettes posted in a colossal crown. We climbed the wild tree and never came down.

United Microclimates

In honor of the air freshener
stripping the atmosphere
of its obscene dew point,
I have a confession I call
The Sand of Cape Cod
Follows Me Home
and an excuse
for each limb of the biting
no-see-em and every
bone in the legs
of the bored blue heron
dragging its clothesline
across our skyscape.
When someone wrote
Amy, R. Is Dead
in morning dew
on the windscreen
I call Terminal Moraine,
I so badly wanted
to rearrange the letters
so that *Amy Is Alive*
shone bright in the a.m.
but I lacked the *V*, the verve,
the *va va voom*, and the wherewithal.
My therapist suspects
an electrolyte imbalance.
Maybe you know
my therapist, the praying mantis
prowling the garden
phlox, searching for a mate
to devour before the first frost.
All this death

is exhausting.
I've missed much
and dropped more,
tripping on rocks,
sun in my eyes.
Today the loveliest breeze
on record scrubbed
the clear veneer
so thoroughly
the weeping willow
swayed east and west
all day until one gust
lifted the tree and
held still its slender
branches for a moment
and from inside the silence
of my living room
I thought
the wind had died
but I was wrong.

Catch & Release

Dear Reluctant Sportsman,
maybe you'll release one
into the watery teeth of the wilds,
a tiny capillary
of our great circulatory system.

Dear Familiar Face
in the Passenger Seat,
I saw you undressing
that comely cornfield.
I agree. Maybe
we're more alike than
our combustible engines
suggest, and if we are,
you hope the next truckstop
has a wedge of rhubarb
pie to die for, too.

Dear Cell Phone Radiation,
we arrive almost invisibly
on the threshold of distant
relatives like a secret cold front,
but our departure demands
much horn honking and
happy hands waving
all the way
to the end
of the on-ramp.
Our relief,
an algorithm
of how lonely
company makes us.

Dear Rainbow Trout,
you're a pretty fish
and I wish we lived
near the shivering brook
and the sunken tree.
Then maybe
we'd finally learn
how to leave
without regret.

Clark's Map

A series of false dichotomies leads to a riverbank, steep and treacherous—a blanket of acorns and wet leaves underfoot. Although wide and presumably deep, the river is still, absent of all ripple, eddy, and wave swirl. The occasional uprooted tree corroborates the current—sometimes a bale of turtles or a pair of coots might be seen basking atop the trunk drifting downstream. What we know is that downstream isn't always down, if down is considered south as it is on this continent. Across the equator it's different, and even here not all rivers flow in one direction. That's not to say snapping turtles can't be identified from shore or that they don't make fine soup despite the dangers of catching them, which is best accomplished by reaching under the bank, down into the holes.

Devil Girl

You send me,
when I'm not trembling
in your vast pumpkin patch,
to investigate the rustling
reeds of autumn and
I find bullfrogs
fucking. It's true
my term in your service
will end one winter solstice.
Until then
I am your soldier,
patrolling the peripheral
vision of the great owls,
searching forests primeval,
my derring-do, for the elusive
shades of chance and circumstance.
When I'm alone
I'm not entirely here
and not entirely alone.
Your horns silhouette
the thorny hedgerow
towering above me.
That sound haunting
my insomnia, is it you
or your god's didgeridoo
calling the wild things
home? It is my only wish
that the power source
to your blustery hydrofoil
commands more than two settings:
Nothing and All.
Still, there's a little me

inside of you, and if
I know myself,
he spends full moons
wading through your swamp,
gig in hand, ear to the wind.
I suspect he's not alone.
In fact the whole big swamp
must be full of waders,
headlamps bobbing in the night.
I can only imagine
what rises with each step,
what darts through the darkness
that separates us two.

A Little Stick

I found this little stick
opposite the yellow maple.
Atop the hill, I stretched
my legs out in the sun and
watched the golden eagles,
one by one, track
their autumnal coordinates
across the blue sky of this daydream.
The tree's shadow, black stencil,
fleur-de-lis, I could see
didn't so much resemble a crooked man
as many gnarly maples do,
but a colossal paisley
upon the lawn.
I twisted the twig
until the red bark shed—
wood in all its nakedness,
knots and holes, light and smooth
like the hollow bones of birds.
A small brown spider crawled
onto my wrist. A whisper
and the spider released
an invisible thread,
which I could see because
I believe in gravity.
On second puff,
the spider released itself
and floated off,
a question.
I picked up the stick
and took it home.
My little one said, *Trees*

grow like hair except different,
and set it on the floor. We didn't
think about our twig anymore
until her mother stepped on it
and said, *Who brought this
stick into the house?* I did,
I did.

Enough Light

To turn the larva in the loam, to buckle
the branches, to break the stone.
Light enough for laws to unmatter
and dirt to have a name. Rain enough
to soak the roots and make them rot,
to drown the fish and make them not.
Wind to murmur husks upon the bark,
to dry wings smooth and make them fly
arboreal lives. World enough to soothe
the buzz and clamor in a forest of hearts.

Island in Dispute Disappears into the Sea

We're not so different
that your north is my south
or my anger is your passion fruit.
Until high tide we saluted
the same royal palm leaning
into a full breeze of birds.
We sacrificed our hammers
and our nails and our paddles
to the same hungry gods,
but that didn't slake their thirst,
nor mine, for I wanted you
to see the green flash of sunset,
and that was only possible
if you truly believed
the sun did set, and you know
the stars better than that.
It's a trick we play on ourselves,
like when we paint
angels on our ceiling.
We see what we know
is not there for fear of falling
from the high ground.
We have communed
with the reef and the volcano,
with the turtle, the tang, and the guava tree,
with the angry young parrots and
the blind who live in caves,
and have come away saying
we knew the heart of the island,
the hearts and minds of the plants
and animals. Slowly like waves
carving beaches out of cliffs,

what we stowed in our amulets,
what made us one, we cleaved in two.
Our dream sank back into the sea.
We are now ten thousand small canoes
bobbing in the chop. With no compass
and no land in sight, we'll wait
for the stars to shine tonight.
Tomorrow comes our sorrow
when we'll finally have
what we wanted,
a country of our own.

What It Is That Abandons You

There is a golden triangle
and in the triangle a tree.
The tree calls, the tree waves,
the tree hunches over the children
and whispers in their ears.
They hear not the deep sap traveling
through their sleeping tendrils.

There is a street. It ignores
the boulevards, the thoroughfares,
the tree. It has no mother, no daughter,
no son. It is a street
whose brick dissolves and intersections
clench and unclench at the cross-
walks like memory's muscle.

There is a square. It is green.
A man has arranged
four windows to face the tree
and two to gaze upon the mountain.
This is his pledge to her.
After the leaves have fallen
she climbs the tree and pulls him up.

This is her gift to him.
When the fruit drops,
the tree shudders,
the triangle roars.

The Four Leaf Blowers of the Apocalypse
Came Calling

I have seen the leaf blowers
and the leaf blowers have seen me,
less leaf-like than waterlogged loafer,
enveloped in a fine plume
of their generous particulate.
Sabotage is a splendid word.
It means with this boot
I thee wed, means
the real Romulus and Remus
behave like split infinitives
under an economic microscope.
Man invented the wheel, the wheel
invented the desire for more,
which invented a new man
and a lazy Susan of wishes.
For generations the leaves just fell,
then one evening I found myself
gathering a handful of species
together on a blank sidewalk.
I gave each leaf a pet name
and then I held them in my forearms
and the smells of autumn attached
themselves to my personal DNA.
Then the steel tines and
the concrete conjured a spark
in the dark, a reminder of the great
generations that burned
their leaves in the autumnal gutters
of yesteryear. As the electric eyes
switched the streetlights on
the girls and boys of Lake City

poured out of their homes
like mad gnomes with automatic shoes
through my pile of perfection
until the melancholy lawn whispered
to the wind, and the wind needed nothing
and could not be made more perfect
and the leaves blew away.

Future Structures

They will build themselves. We will call them green buildings. They
will breathe, they will perspire. Their roofs will be fields of winter
wheat. Their windows, semi-permeable membranes. They'll grow like
coral reefs and resemble hills and mountains, so much so the hills
and mountains will forgive our trespass. As these future structures
respire, the emptiness within will meet the emptiness without. The
parched tree will find a spring and a flock of crows will lift from their
perch in one great semaphore. This will mark the end of modern
architecture as we have come to call our dream.

Collective Hum

I was relieved really
when I read, learned
there was no human species,
or rather human species
represents a categorical error,
one abused by a belief
in progress, that slow
precipitating crystal
on which hippodromes squat
and imperfect engines run.
We all know our human beings.
We call them people,
usually, sometimes rats,
pigs, snakes, sheep.
There are millions
and billions of us.
We are a Malthusian wave
swamping the jagged shore
of a blue-green island in space,
a swarm of individuals
atomized in free air,
an anthill decapitated
by the lawn boy.
My relief lies
in my little faith in myself
to overcome biology.
There's no shame in that.
The contents of the formicary
disperse like a ragged Doppler,
then the waves contract
and the ants return
to their loamy womb

carrying broken bodies.
Mandibles, antennae,
defensive anus,
hardwired with hardware,
order makes the ant
an ant. That's
not to say
I haven't been
or will be
a great insect
society.

What Your T-Shirt Says about Me

Yesterday wasn't great
blue herons working their way
over crocus-covered hills
and then gliding down to the marsh
below, but maybe today.
Maybe today we'll recognize one another
in the thick accent of our eyeglasses
or the culture of our crooked gait.

Tuesday resembled a bucket of ice,
not a thousand ice cubes glistening
in the sun of exotic refreshment
but a solid ice-block bucket
and at the bottom a lithe ladle
reclining on its side, proud
of its perfect blue hips
and I was thirsty.

Maybe today
the adrenalin junkie
with the wild leg will come
humming up High Street
like the morning
we were two magnificent birds
escaping separate but
equally pedestrian fates.
With each step we became more alike
until the gothic letters of her shirt

came into view and I saw
deep into the serif of her capitals,
a country whose black forest surrounds

the tomb of the unknowns and whose
state bird remains the dodo.
A whirl of wordlessness and then
before us, the uneven
sidewalk of tomorrow
whose slogans are unwritten
and will remain so.

Dear Advertorial Board

Bite and smile
remains your best work.
My mouth gets wet
thinking about it.

Burger A & Burger B
stand united
as pleasure principles,
gateways to the west.

Remember Stalin.
His outstanding
moustache and the swagger
stick. That's branding.

Copy is a kind of poetry
that sends you whistling
erectile dysfunction at sunset
and singing hallelujah soda

in trucks man enough
to change the world,
one diaper at a time,
not like the schmuck

cowed in the ballot box,
the two tribes of loathing,
traditional and extra-crunchy,
waiting their turn.

Hitler invented the people's
car, but not daylight savings

as many believe,
which is propaganda

working overtime.
The truth is
I am brand loyal
and I choose

the unregistered beauty
of a bowl of soup and
tumbleweeds on the street
to cure the empty cavity

I call my own.

Please, She Said

Mistaking commands
for requests can make
for happy accidents,
unspoken symbiosis,
if you will. Take a moment
and notice the shrubbery,
the pulse behind your knee,
the plane your sole
touches, the earth.
You are in a large diffuse field,
part of the field is dying.
You may be that part.
Elsewhere, exotic quadrant,
black staffs of antennae,
ants shepherd aphids
plump with chartreuse translucence,
honeydew, nectar, elixir of wife.
This is their currency, their contract.
For sweet sustenance, provide
shelter for our soft, fragile bodies
for as long as we both shall live
well. She said the arborvitae
means the porch isn't plumb
and the foundation sank
long before the time capsule
hemorrhaged in the ticktock of twilight,
and the carpenter will not rise again.
Mothballs, in addition,
planted in the tulip bed
indicate the Bavarian hag
hates rabbits roaming wild
more than the smell of death.

The equations, tell me,
echo like empty rooms
without numbers
and shelter dilated
orphans with them.
Mistake request
for command
and make an enemy
out of love
and the neighbor slowly
denuding maples
in the rain.

All Over Town

Minneapolis
either means city of the lakes
or Prince's *Purple Rain*.

Everything happens
for a reason or because
everything happens.

Minneapolis
either means city of the lakes
or drunk on the moon.

Welcome back, grackle.
The snow has melted and left you
mittens for your nest.

Morning Ornithology

Our patriotic pantaloons made us more like birds and less
like flying machines and we were thankful, for the capital is
a golden dome of horses and many splendid trees line the way.

We ruminated about what the state bird means
elsewhere and what state precisely we were entering
and which we had abandoned to roadkill and firecracker stands.

The state gemstone resembles a piece of the moon.
Under glass the glorious clod emanates a hum,
sounds like an idea thrumming underwater.

We're lucky the fair compares blackberry crumble and red meat,
lucky the winning cookies look exactly like the losing cookies.
Yet we must imagine their deliciousness, we must lick our lips

and suck our tongues. If we create our own state, may the birds
circle not our capital but perch and peck and show us their teeth
when we forget how close the moon is and how sweet the air can be.

Falling Back into the Sky

A stucco exterior can be a section
or an extension of the sky.
The silence conjured by the clouds says so.
Last night or the night before
I bumped my head on a window grate
in the courtyard of Santo Spirito
and the Dirty Needles.
I wanted an aerial view,
a dotted line following us
through the walled city—a big black *X*
where two trains of thought collided.
Somewhere in the gray matter
it's written in wet chalk,
Apply cold compress to contusion.
Had the gorgeous Romans been more
reluctant to share their ice,
a warm rag would've had to suffice.
The cells say also,
a concussion invites coma,
sleep at your own risk.
Love lay beside me,
left to wonder what is sleep
and what is what.
Even the gypsies
clustered by the Duomo
declined to pilfer my pockets.
Near Ponte Vecchio,
draped over the Arno's neck
like a gaudy bauble,
we found vintage graffiti
on the back of a tobacco shop.
Between the shadows

of Michelangelo and Galileo,
(Ohio)
hung over the sidewalk,
like *will you* script in the sky with smoke.
This was a sign.
Our people see stars
when we bang our heads
or that's what we call pain
flashing in the night behind our eyes.
We've glided over the outer banks,
circled earth and touched the moon
where our footprints refuse to die.
This too is a sign.

Until

I saw the tub overflow with moonlight
like it did last night when I got up
to listen to the green walls
because I thought some wild thing
was building a nest behind
the boards separating us
from the out of doors.
I never knew light was an accident
or that night holds us
in its hands
like smoke until

we're gone.

A Continuing Education

If you have ever dug a grave
        in Minnesota
                on the winter solstice,

you know death
        is harder on the living
                than the dead, harder

than the dumb sod blunting
        the spade's sparkling tip.
                Such wisdom stinks.

If the ground under
        the apple is a knot,
                unyielding to the nail,

then move closer, nearer
        the foundation
                where white coneflowers

smolder in the spring,
        where the earth is soft and warmer
                than it ought to be, and dig.

If the sky, slung low, groans
        gray with snow, look up
                and forget your chore

for a moment. If the crows traffic
        toward their evening roost,
                then winter's long night

is about to descend. Before
      snow fulfills your silent task
           and Ice on eyelashes

hangs haloes on streetlamps,
      know death is a pledge
           we try not to keep, a lesson

we can't help learning the hard way.

The Allness & Infinity of Barber Shops

Not unlike the great
grandfather of your wide-
angle lens, mine had
a splendid head,
a root ball of fine
dark strands,
and so blessed
he dreamed
up a barbershop
by a railroad stop,
had a son
who learned to walk
between the Lucky Tiger
and Golden Buddha,
bottles shimmering
like forgotten jewels
in the mild afternoon,
and named him Harry.
The trees were there,
bursting deep buds of the sea.
Naturally Harry
took to cutting locks
and did so for years.
Along the way
he caught himself
combing and clipping
in the mirror,
looking a stranger.
Then a son too
and the world
grew stranger still
and off to Normandy

his only son did sail.
It wasn't long
before the barber
business sank
back into the sea.
The son returned
from a world at war,
married a young lily
of the valley from Montana,
and fathered two sons,
one a Marine,
one something else.
The jarhead lost
his hair somewhere
between Europe
and the Euphrates.
The other keeps his
short and unkempt
and has a daughter
with auburn curls.
I take her to Les's
Hair Police North-
east. She watches
from behind a shabby
Archie & Jughead
as the barber
and I reestablish
our common ground,
a muddy footpath
along the mighty
Mississippi where punks
toss plastic bottles

at pileated woodpeckers.
I'm sorry, Les is an ass,
but not his partner Art,
who's a real Texas gentleman,
despite carousing
in Juarez every Easter.
Les owns the place:
mirrors, chairs,
razors, everything.
If there were a pole,
he'd own that.
I miss those lazy spirals,
beacons of beginnings
and ancient bloodletting.
A good cut gets better
then goes to seed,
summer dandelion.
Barbers are either talkers
or failures. A laconic man
with a razor is bad business.
I'll take my chances
on bad cuts and
the rants of bitter men.
Les runs a sportsbook
and a casino excursion
out of a cigar box
under the slop sink.
Sportsbook makes
a bookie feel
like an artist of sorts.
Les photographs the
regulars and tapes them

'round an Old Faithful
panorama. If you're patient
you'll find me,
my portrait,
among a gallery
of old men in smocks.
If I look surprised
it's because Les
ambushed me.
He got busted once
so the mayor
calls in advance
to catch Art alone.
The mayor's in a green
party, which one
I can't be sure.
A barber will reveal
his affiliations
to the hum of clippers.
Les is a Republican,
the kind that picks
the leaves before they fall.
Art is a dancer
and ladies like his moves.
Last spring he returned
with the ruby-throated
hummingbirds carrying
a flesh eating virus.
They're hard to catch.
My daughter and I often
spot him on the limestone
bridge. We watch

the falls together,
the churning turbines
of water and momentum,
the frothy head of time
drifting downstream.
There's no telling
when a great weeping
willow will tumble
down the cataracts,
a clumsy cartwheel of
doom. I try to imagine
the falls no more
before my daughter
takes my hand and stops
my cascade, pointing
to a black cormorant,
and asks, *What do you
think of swimming birds?*
Art offers an orange
candy I didn't know
existed. He keeps walking
toward the mill ruins.
The last time
he drove to Mexico,
he toured a charm
bracelet of towns.
He shows off snapshots
of his dancehall dames,
the young ladies
of Matamoras
and San Miguel
de Allende. Art is

Casanova reborn,
an odd octogenarian.
For my first haircut,
all the adults
wore toothy smiles,
though gravity
perfumed the air
conditioned room
like burning leaves.
I could tell
we were to believe
things would never
be the same.
The barber's voice
faded as I
faced the mirror.
It wasn't my reflection
that fascinated but the ping
pong of images between
the mirrors, front and back,
the infinite accordion play
between them, a picture within
a picture within a picture
until a magnifying glass was needed
to see the next reproduction
and then a microscope
to bring forever into focus.
They were right,
though it wasn't the lost
curls of boyhood innocence,
accumulating on the linoleum
like fallen leaves,

but my first brush
with infinity.
My best cut found me
honeymooning
in San Gimignano.
My Italian was good
enough to fool the tourists
who photographed me
atop my hydraulic
chariot like a real Roman.
I admire Art
for leaving Minnesota
in the winter, for traveling
alone at eighty.
Like the kestrel
next door, one spring
he won't come back
and I'll be left with Les
until I quit
cutting my hair
or my hair quits me.
Now when I look
into Art's mirror,
which is like snapping
a photo of a river,
I see a certain idea of myself,
and if I look harder,
I see my father and his
father, and if I look again,
I see my daughter.
One day the barbershop door
clicked open and

in rushed spring.
I looked to see a shy boy
wiping his red sneakers
on the welcome mat.
Then I caught my daughter,
the real one, the one waiting
there in a roomful of men,
the one with curious eyes,
watching me, and then she glanced
back toward the glass
door, which offered all
the trees and birds of the world
and reflected the whole
barbershop stock-still,
each of us peering out
quietly from the inside,
not unlike the Milky Way.

A Part of It

We stowed the dark map
in its long, dark cylinder.
The night was complete,
all the stars and planets named,
arranged, fables for the future
now twinkling on our table of bitters.
Someone's son, yours,
the one with eyes of the wilderness,
submitted that your coordinates
lay amid a constellation,
the one we call the Shy Antelope of Sorrow,
whose story knows a beginning
forgotten, and an end fixed,
a knot hung from the ceiling.
All of us are together
in our forlorn skins.
It's why comfort's found
in fall's low-slung clouds,
why we crowd the night sky
with animals whose glinty eyes
keep us company. Sometimes
we choose to believe
our lies.

And Everything Else

Bill has a face
he wants to share.
Bill has a phantom
limb he'd like to pet.
Bill is updating his mythology,
his mythology is updating him.
Bill likes horses at night,
moonlight rippling in their eyes
like spoons of milk.
Bill likes hummingbirds
in flight. Bill wishes
he were a delicate petal.
Bill ponders cloud shadows,
the dark fields they tend
like shallow wounds.
Bill is a one-man assembly line.
Bill knows a little history.
Bill remembers Otto Dix.
Bill bought dynamite in
Manitoba and hung
crumpled exclamations
over the landscape.
Bill is an attractive nuisance.
Bill is a fan of a Portuguese poet
who goes by many names.
Bill shows off
and circumnavigates.
Bill is a book and
he says we're in it
until the lights go out.
Bill admires amphibians,
the soft pulse of their throats.

Bill is distracted.
Bill lost a button
in a field of drunken flowers.
Bill feels fine now.
Bill wants to be friends.
Bill is a fearless bird.
Watch him soar.
Bill is La Crosse in a canoe.
Bill seeks approval.
Bill flirted with a lilac and lost.
Bill wonders what
a white squirrel portends.
Bill is a clean window
on a sunny day. Bill is a hill
in Ohio. Bill footnotes
today, essays tomorrow.
Bill is in the future.
Bill is pleased to report
the arrival of now.

Prevailing Westerly

I don't know why
Dusty Baker is Dusty Baker.
I don't know why
anyone is anyone.
I do know we all come from
somewhere bittersweet,
more cocoa than confection,
a place that squats
in our cells long
after we've moved on,
long after Dusty waited on deck
for Hank Aaron to come home.
The flag flying over Baker,
Montana is a cloud of prehistoric dust,
part Bitterroot, part Yellowstone,
part mastodon, part radio transmision.

Sneaky Gene

We live in the forest. We have always lived in the forest. The trees are our brothers and our sisters. Some believe our mother was a miraculous plum, heavy with fruit, and that is why we are fructivores, but they are mistaken. The river of mysterious origins separates us from our origin, and when the forest closes with darkness like a blossom, the ache of a bitter nut fills our maws and our throats tighten. For a moment, the whole world is still, suspended from the sky by threads of starlight. But this passes and we swing from trees again thanks to the grand order of pollinators and the new moon for such freedom, if such freedom exists.

One night I taught a coconut to sing and the note was thud in the mud of the jungle floor and thus our communion broke into shards. Almost invisible on the edge of our grove, no one saw my toss. The silent cup inside the coconut falling made me think of the forbidden clearing, so I snuck off after the others had retired to their leafy embraces, through the underbrush, past calls of the unknown and the unnamed, until I came to the last tree and crept lizard-like from the canopy and I looked up at the starry dome and knew next time I would not come alone.

We Pilgrims Piggybacked the River, Instinct Puffy in Our Eyes

The Queen City may have shimmered
mildly on the far shore,
but Newport is for foraging
and thus attractive in deformity.
A black eye's black stye
served alternative tentacles,
which we devoured, slowly
disassembling the unhistory
we'd memorized so dutifully.
Then the sound of fresh fruit
bursting over the throng
of rotting vegetables moved us,
damp and undulating, and one
by one by none we jackknifed
upstage. Entangled
in a snare of cords and cables,
Jello gently unnetted me.
Floating there
before the crescendo
I wanted to be
more than anything.
Then the surge and swell
passed me back,
a beatific insect
atop a mass of army ants.
Glasses lost amid the jubilee
until the last chord reverberated
in the four chambers of our hearts,
and although my astigmatism
is worse now,
my vision is not.

My Information

Later, when it's dark
I'll crash the gate
(security),
I'll jump the shark
(hammerhead),
I'll sneak into the grizzly lair
(artificial)
and sext her
there (traditional).
I'll graffiti the phony
tree (mulberry)
the bear (sun)
rubs his rump on.
I'm not sure what I'll say,
but I promise
not to disgrace
the human race.
One day I'd like to feel
Egyptian hieroglyphs
(X-rated)
and to admire what
Lewis & Clark scrawled
on the river bluffs
(dates, initials)
as they navigated
a reluctant continent.
But in the meantime
please delete me
from your database
for my name is my own
and my whereabouts
shall remain unknown
to all but the breeze.

On the Warp Path

Tell me something
I need to know.
Tell me why the Great
Lakes are lonesome
for whales, why the night
sky apes an archipelago
caught in a navy net,
why islands look
like stars from the sea.
Did we build our shack
on sacred ground, did the trees
erase a serpent mound,
did the snake entomb a billion
seeds and spent embers,
did the flames crawl
over slag and bones
unknown? Tell me how
the black bear grows
fat on berries and grubs
and blue whales eat their fill
of krill and we remain runts
on pig meat. How do we
do what we do
with such small brains
and even smaller hands?
How in the world
will we find our way
along this bent path
with only the light
we carry.

Calculus Accumulates Upon the Mighty Cuspids

Nine out of ten dentists dream
white armies of scrimshaw gods.
Their bent instruments doze
in snowy imperfection.
Is anything more divine
than bacteria building
cathedrals of forever?
Numbers unflower
in mountain tinctures
and stellar eulogies.
Nine out of ten dentists
dream their hygienists
who dream trains and stops
and flopping uvulas,
human lacuna, box of amnesia.
When she slides
the second hand in
I feel almost complete
in my incompleteness.
Stars are born in nurseries
and die alone.
She inserts a sprinkler
and irrigates the sockets.
My tongue follows her latex digits.
Gasps are half swallowed words.
I blood my spit and down it swirls.
It goes unspoken,
the hygienist and I
will never be unhappy
together. In the mountains,
it's snowing.
Our bones are buried there.

I'll Be the One Wearing Tiny White Boots

In hell,
in hell there's one
season. It's called cold
cruel oatmeal but it's never
too soon to wear white slacks,

white hats,
white socks, white jocks.
Sundays we fling our javelins
into the mystery down by the river
while the feted ferries come in. *Toot Toot.*

We're concerned
less with accuracy than distance.
May this toss take me elsewhere, may
the breeze off Fire Lake carry, may these boots
move me and if not, make me happy here.

In memory of Fred J. Waltz (1923-2007)